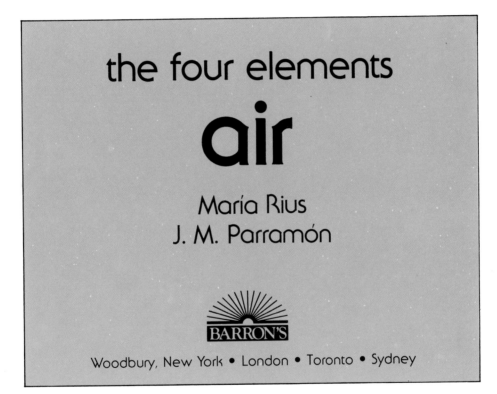

the four elements
air

María Rius
J. M. Parramón

BARRON'S

Woodbury, New York • London • Toronto • Sydney

You don't see it, but it moves.

It's called a *breeze* when it caresses.

a *wind* when it bothers you,

and a *hurricane* when it destroys.

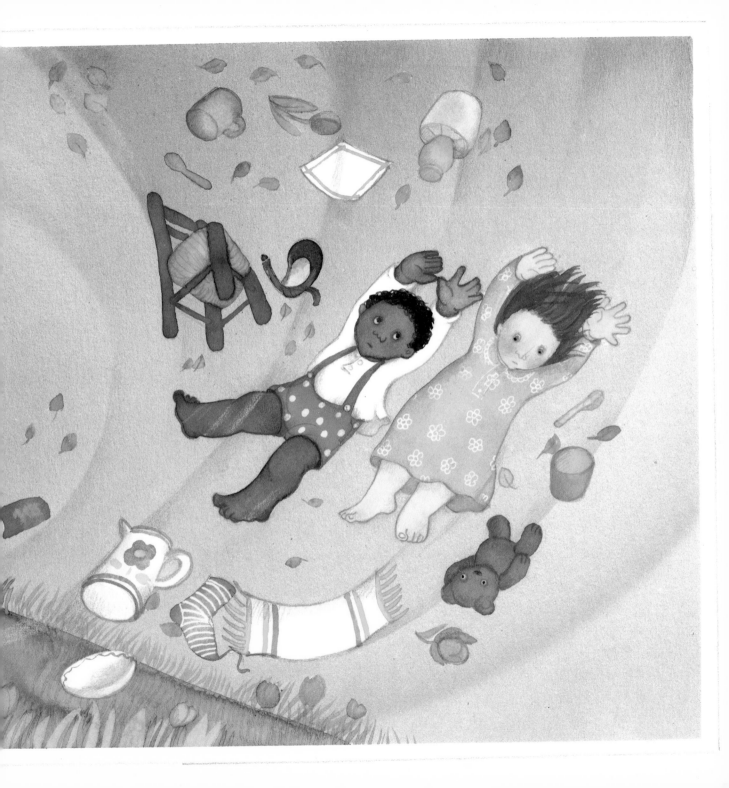

It has the power to raise a kite...

...to make a balloon fly...

...to move the sails of a windmill...

...to push a boat...

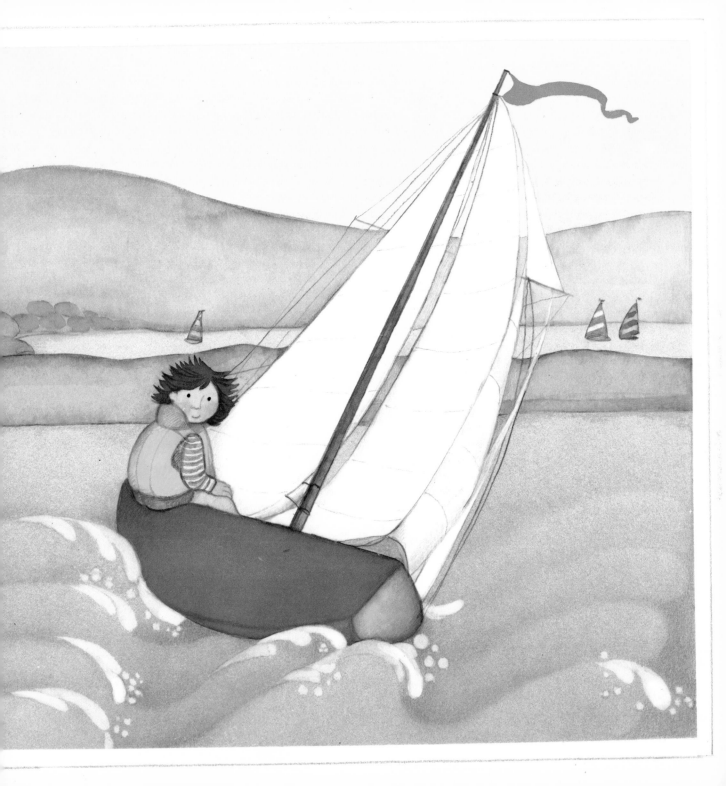

...to hold up a plane...

...to let birds fly...

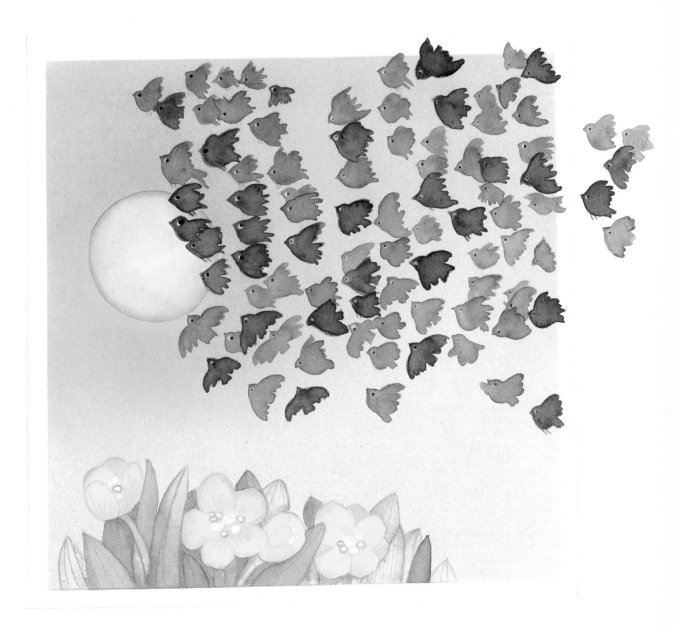

...to let a man come down from the sky...

...to let you and your animals and your plants breathe...and live!

IT'S AIR!

AIR

"A I R
A I - R
A - I R
A - I - R"

The air that surrounds us

You can't see it, you can't touch it, but it's there. It's what shakes the branches of the trees, lifts up skirts, ruffles your hair.

It's what you put in a football or a bicycle tire. Air can be compressed. The ball regains its shape after a kick. Air is elastic. When a car tire is punctured, the air escapes, it spreads. How far?

Does air end?

Imagine that air is formed by tiny balls that move in every direction without stopping, bumping into each other and against the wall of the container that holds them. Air surrounds us.

But air doesn't scatter through interplanetary space because the force of gravity pulls on each of the little balls. Air has weight. The thickness of the layer of air that surrounds the earth (the atmosphere) is about seven hundred miles.

The weight of the air at the earth's surface is called *atmospheric pressure*. Where is this pressure the greatest? At the top of a mountain or at sea level? As we go up, the air becomes less dense and the atmospheric pressure decreases, so the support layer of air is thinner. On a very high mountain you will find it difficult to breathe.

The air we breathe

You couldn't stand being underwater for a long time: you need air to breathe. You aren't like fish who can absorb the oxygen dissolved in the water.

The air is composed of about one-fifth oxygen and four-fifths nitrogen, plus some other substances.

Oxygen is indispensable in all combustion. Therefore, if you have a lit candle and you cover it with a glass container, you'll see that after a little while it will go out. Most of the oxygen has been consumed!

In the olden days they called nitrogen "azoe" from the Greek *a* (negation) and *zoe* (life), because with only nitrogen the candle would go out and the animals would die. But its presence is important biologically. Some microscopic bacteria, living in the soil, are capable of using nitrogen from the air to make nitrate compounds, which are necessary for plant development.

When you take a cold bottle from the refrigerator, little drops appear on the outside of the bottles. What are they? These little drops are water that are found in the air in the form of vapor, which has condensed upon contact with a cold surface.

In small and varying proportions, there are other gases in the air, such as water vapor and carbon dioxide, the gas produced by your body in respiration, and products formed by many combustions, such as the gas we cook with. In the presence of light,